D0998665

Bread and Grains

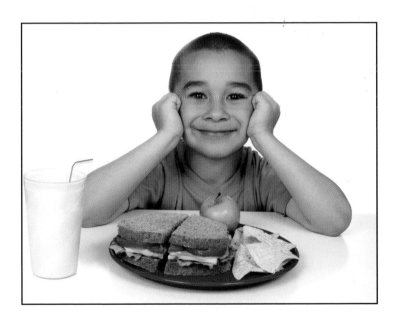

D.H. Dilkes

Enslow Elementary

an imprint of

Enslow Publishers, Inc.

40 Industrial Road
Box 398
Berkeley Heights, NJ 07922
USA

http://www.enslow.com

For my girls: Nicole, Jocelynn, and Devynn

Enslow Elementary, an imprint of Enslow Publishers, Inc.
Enslow Elementary® is a registered trademark of Enslow Publishers, Inc.

Library of Congress Cataloging-in-Publication Data

Dilkes, D. H.
  Bread and grains / D.H. Dilkes.
      p. cm. — (All about good foods we eat)
  Includes bibliographical references and index.
  Summary: "Introduces bread and grains in everyday meals to pre-readers using repetition of words and short, simple sentences with photos and illustrations to enhance the text"—Provided by publisher.
  ISBN 978-0-7660-3923-0
  1. Bread—Juvenile literature. 2. Grain—Juvenile literature. I. Title.
  TX769.D55 2012
  641.8'15—dc23   2011015673

Paperback ISBN 978-1-59845-252-5

Printed in the United States of America
052011 Lake Book Manufacturing, Inc., Melrose Park, IL

10 9 8 7 6 5 4 3 2 1

To Our Readers: We have done our best to make sure all Internet Addresses in this book were active and appropriate when we went to press. However, the author and the publisher have no control over and assume no liability for the material available on those Internet sites or on other Web sites they may link to. Any comments or suggestions can be sent by e-mail to comments@enslow.com or to the address on the back cover.

✪ Enslow Publishers, Inc., is committed to printing our books on recycled paper. The paper in every book contains 10% to 30% post-consumer waste (PCW). The cover board on the outside of each book contains 100% PCW. Our goal is to do our part to help young people and the environment too!

Photo Credits: Shutterstock.com

Cover Photo: Shutterstock.com

Note to Parents and Teachers

Help pre-readers get a jumpstart on reading. These lively stories introduce simple concepts with repetition of words and short simple sentences. Photos and illustrations fill the pages with color and effectively enhance the text. Free Educator Guides are available for this series at www.enslow.com. Search for the *All About Good Foods We Eat* series name.

Warning: The foods in this book may contain ingredients to which people may be allergic, such as peanuts and milk.

Contents

Words to Know

syrup   **tortilla**   **waffle**

I am having cornflakes
for breakfast.

They taste good
with milk.

I am having waffles
for breakfast.

They taste good
with syrup.

I am having a sandwich for lunch.

I made it with wheat bread.

I am having a wrap for lunch.

I made it with a tortilla.

I am eating dinner.

There is rice on
my plate.

I am eating my dinner.

There is pasta on
my plate.

My family likes popcorn.
It is a healthy snack.

I like crackers for
a snack.

They are good plain
or in soup.

Corn muffins are
tasty and sweet.

I eat them for dessert.

I am eating my dessert.

An oatmeal cookie
hits the spot!

Read More

Burstein, John. *Glorious Grains*. New York: Crabtree Pub., 2010.

Kalz, Jill. *Grains*. North Mankato, Minn.: Smart Apple Media, 2003.

Web Sites

PBS Kids: *Sid the Science Kid* Mix it Up
<http://pbskids.org/sid/mixitup.html>
Help Sid create a balanced meal!

Smallstep Kids: MyPyramid Blast Off
<http://teamnutrition.usda.gov/Resources/game/BlastOff_Game.
    html>
A fun game that teaches the food pyramid.

Index

Guided Reading Level: D
Guided Reading Leveling System is based on the guidelines
recommended by Fountas and Pinnell.

Word Count: 114